SCHIRMER'S LIBRARY
OF MUSICAL CLASSICS

Vol. 1179

T0210264

J. DONT

Op. 35

Twenty-Four
Études and Caprices

For the Violin

ISBN 978-0-7935-5221-4

G. SCHIRMER, Inc.

DISTRIBUTED BY

HAL•LEONARD®
CORPORATION
7777 W. BLUEMOUND RD. P.O. BOX 13819 MILWAUKEE, WI 53213

PREFACE

* * * * * *

The Viennese violinist Jakob Dont (1815-1888) was far better known as a teacher than as a performer. He was, indeed, one of the great teachers of the 19th century. One of his pupils was Leopold Auer, the renowned Russian violinist and teacher. In addition to his activities as a pedagogue, Dont found time to write a number of books of first-class studies, two of which— "24 Exercises Preparatory to Kreutzer" and "24 Etudes and Caprices"—are used today wherever the violin is seriously taught.

In his studies Dont anticipated to a large degree what is now known as the "modern" technique of fingering. In editing these Etudes and Caprices, I have endeavored to develop Dont's original ideas in the light of later technical advances.

In general, these Etudes promote accuracy, solidity, and strength of finger more than they develop left-hand facility. Furthermore, there is not much material for the building of a varied bow-technique. It is well, therefore, to combine them with studies that call for left-hand fluency and right-arm agility, such as the "First Thirty Concert Studies" by De Bériot. However, in spite of these seeming shortcomings, they are essential to the training of the ambitious student, for they bear the same relationship to advanced violin playing that the Kreutzer studies bear to intermediate technique.

No metronome markings were originally given. Those in the present edition represent a goal to be attained, not the speed at which the various studies should be practised.

The square, open notes which appear in several of the Etudes—e.g. the first measure of No. 2 —indicate Advance Fingering; that is, the placing of a finger on a string in preparation for a note that will be played a moment or so later. After this principle has become a part of subconscious left-hand technique, a considerable gain in solidity will be noticed in all passage-work, and— because of the elimination of many separate finger-movements—rapidity of fingering will be greatly advanced.

* * * * * *

Caprice No. 1. To gain technical mastery, it is well to practise this difficult study in the following manner, slowly:

When the notes are mastered, the chords should be played with alternate Down and Up bows as well as with all Down bows.

Caprice No. 2. To be played with a broad yet buoyant détaché stroke in the upper half of the bow, marking the accents strongly. A finished performance of this study should have a fiery impetuosity. Practised détaché in the lower half of the bow, it is useful for developing a flexible bow arm.

Caprice No. 3. A first-class study for intonation and for developing an equalized finger pressure. It should be practised both détaché and legato. When legato, the technique of Round Bowing* must be observed. After the notes are well learned, the study may be played spiccato. In all bowings, the rise and fall of the upper arm should have careful attention.

*See Harold Berkley: "The Modern Technique of Violin Bowing", Chap. V. Published by G. Schirmer, Inc., New York.

Caprice No. 4. The chords should be arpeggiated as little as possible. The *piano* sections are best taken in the middle third of the bow, the second sixteenth of each pair being sounded by itself. More bow is needed in the *forte* sections, and the middle note of each chord is sustained with the second sixteenth.

Caprice No. 5. It is advisable to finger the broken intervals as though they were double-stops; i.e., stopping the second note of each pair as the first note is being stopped. This makes for technical accuracy. The rise and fall of the bow must be well controlled. Exaggeration of this movement is a common fault when strings are alternately played. At a rapid tempo, the forearm should move as if only one string were being used, the wrist alone being responsible for string crossings. The varied dynamics are best produced by increasing or decreasing the length of the bow stroke.

The object of the fingering in line 7, measure 1, group 2, and similar measures, is to facilitate the playing of the tenth by moving the hand into the position halfway between the two notes of the interval.

Caprice No. 6. Perhaps the finest short-trill study available to the advanced violinist, this Caprice can do much to develop the strength and independence of the fingers. At first, the student should take care not to sacrifice strength to speed.

Caprice No. 7. An outstanding study for intonation and one that can aid greatly in developing an instinctive "finger-board sense". As the notes are learned, the evenness of the legato should have increasingly more attention. See note to Caprice No. 5 with regard to the alternation of strings and also with regard to the prepared fingering for the tenths.

Caprice No. 8. This Caprice should be practised daily until it can be played fluently and easily. It is especially valuable for those students who do not bring the left hand sufficiently around in the playing of double-stops.

Caprice No. 9. To be played in the lower half of the bow. The chords call for crisp articulation, the bow leaving the strings. The trills need a slight accent to give them brilliance.

Caprice No. 10. As an exercise in the stopping of four-part chords, the value of this study is obvious. To make the most of it, the student should endeavor to stop the notes of each chord simultaneously. Dont's original bowing is shown beneath the notes of the first group. Its value to the modern violinist is doubtful. More practical is the bowing given above the notes; it should be taken in the lower third of the bow, which leaves the strings very slightly after each stroke. The Wrist-and-Finger Motion* should be used throughout.

Caprice No. 11. The melodic line, whether it lies in the highest or the lowest notes of the chords, must be clearly brought out. When the melody is in the lowest notes it should be practised in the following ways: (a) by taking the low note fractionally ahead of the other notes, and (b) in this manner:

Caprice No. 12. This study needs little comment, except to call attention to the staccato eighths and the sustained quarters. It is better to divide the slurs into three bows until the notes are learned.

---

*Ibid: Chapter III

Caprice No. 13. The consistent use of Advance Fingering will aid in gaining technical mastery. The bowing is a vigorous martelé except where legato is indicated.

Caprice No. 14. The left-hand difficulties in this study cannot be taken lightly, but they are entirely violinistic and will quickly yield to conscientious practice. To get an even balance of tone between the two strings in the legato double-stops will require concentrated attention. The *piano* chords can be arpeggiated slightly, but the *forte* chords should be taken as firmly as possible.

Caprice No. 15. Each short trill needs a pronounced bow accent. The sixteenths which follow the trills should not be played too short; each should receive a strong finger grip and a quick, intense vibrato.

Caprice No. 16. The first two measures, and many similar measures, are difficult to play in tune because of the hidden augmented fourth between the third and fourth eighths. This point needs close attention. The study as a whole is a test of the player's intonation.

Caprice No. 17. The first-finger shift is the most frequent of all shifts, and few studies deal with it adequately. This study should be practised and re-practised until it can be played fluently and accurately at the indicated tempo. The left elbow must be well under the violin throughout.

Caprice No. 18. An excellent study for promoting a correct shaping of the hand in the lower positions.

Caprice No. 19. For the purpose of acquiring accurate intonation, this study is better practised with the same figuration and with the same bowing that was recommended for No. 10. To develop the sautillé arpeggio* bowing the variants should be studied in the order in which they are given.

Caprice No. 20. The spiccato indication had better be ignored at first and the study played with a broad détaché until the notes are mastered. When the left-hand technique is secure, the spiccato can be used to great advantage. This study is especially valuable for improving fluency in shifting.

Caprice No. 21. This is a first-class intonation study and is equally useful for promoting a correct shaping of the hand in shifting. The student must take care that the third and fourth fingers stop the strings simultaneously on the first sixteenth of the second group and all similar passages. The tendency is for the third finger to reach its string ahead of the fourth.

Caprice No. 22. There are many technical problems here, all of which require careful thought. For the right hand, the accents on the trills, the smoothness of the legato despite the awkward shifts, and, on the second page, the frequent skips to the G string, all need great care. For the left hand, the shifts, the many modulations, and the passages in tenths and diminished sevenths call for the attention of a keen and critical ear. The dynamics must be carefully observed.

Caprice No. 23. Until the notes are learned, the following bowing is recommended:

In the first three lines and similar passages the student's aim should be to place his fingers on all

*Ibid: Chapter VII

notes of the chords simultaneously.   More than most of these studies, this is a preview of the technique required for the Paganini Caprices, and it should be studied with this goal in view.

Caprice No. 24.   The only study in the book that calls for a varied musical expression—a difficult task considering the technical problems that confront the player.   First, of course, the technique must be mastered, then the appropriate expression merged with it.   For it is one of the hall-marks of the true artist that he can play difficult technical passages with the color and expressive qualities he gives to a simple melodic line.

New York, 1952   HAROLD BERKLEY

Twenty-four
Études and Caprices

□ Down-Bow
V Up-Bow

Jakob Dont, Op. 35
Edited by Harold Berkley

remain in position _ _ _ _ _

Allegretto scherzando ♪= 92

4

dim. e poco rit.

Allegro appassionato ♩. = 80

5

6

Allegretto scherzoso ♪= 100

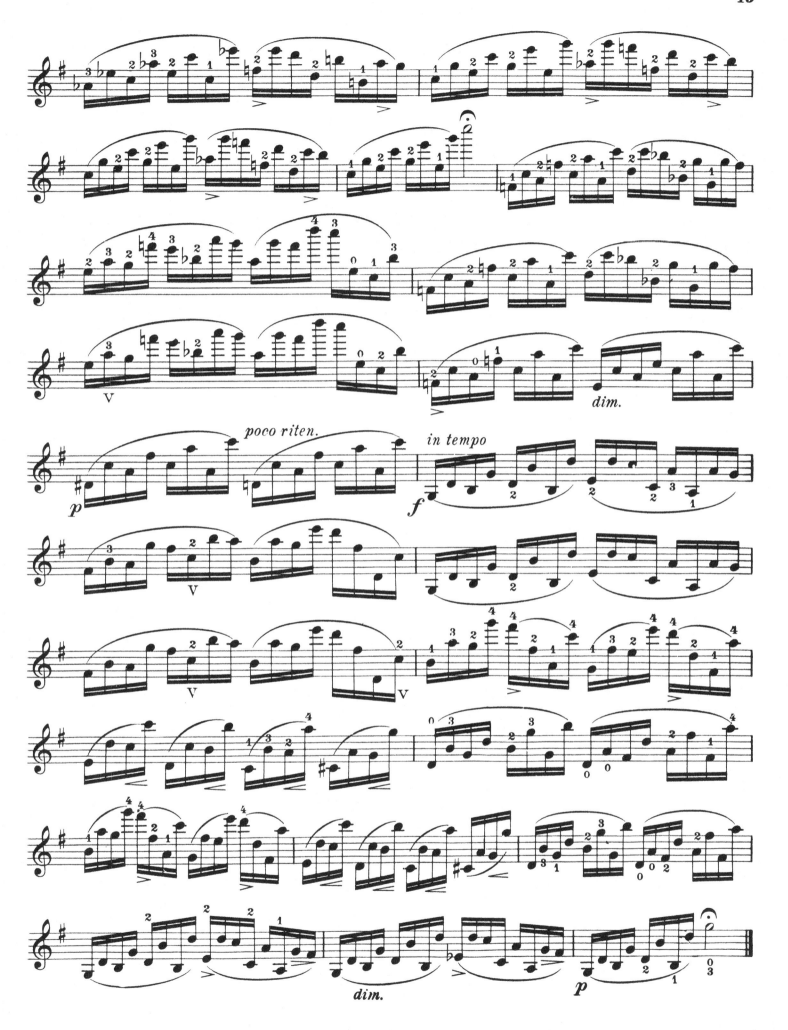

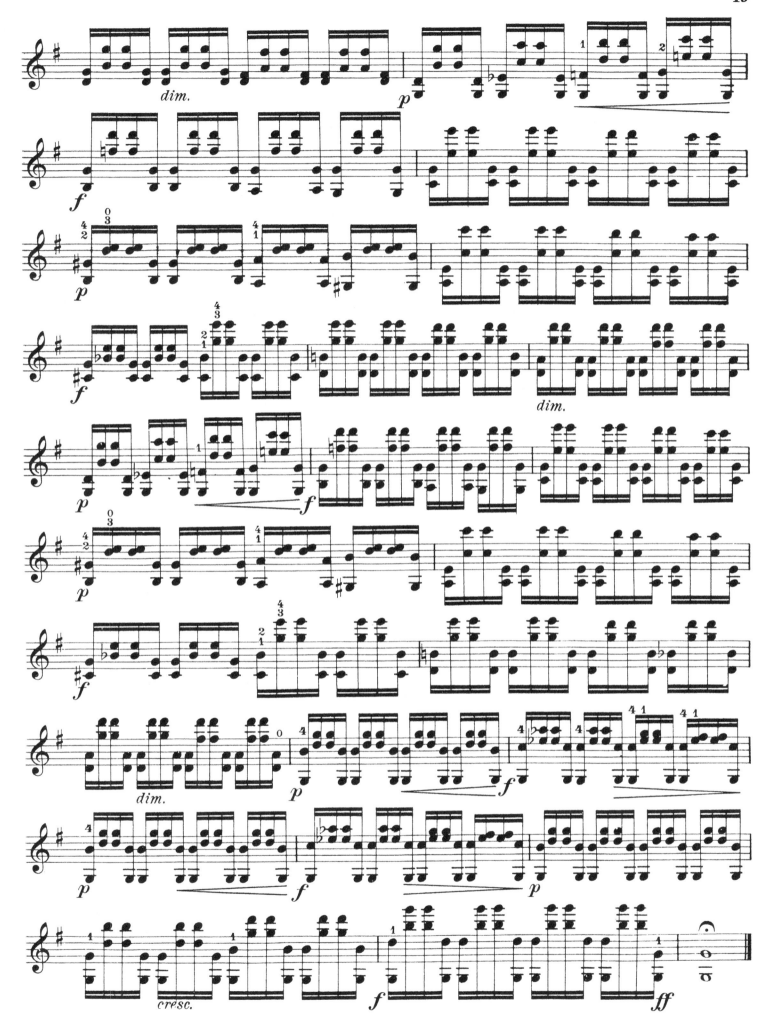

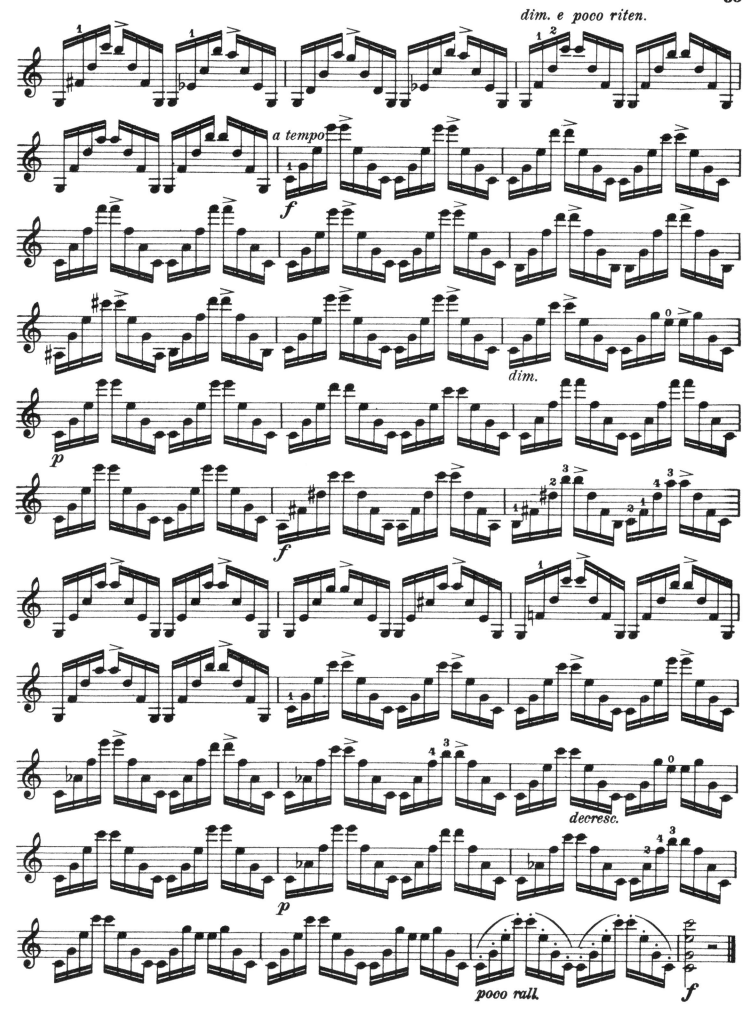

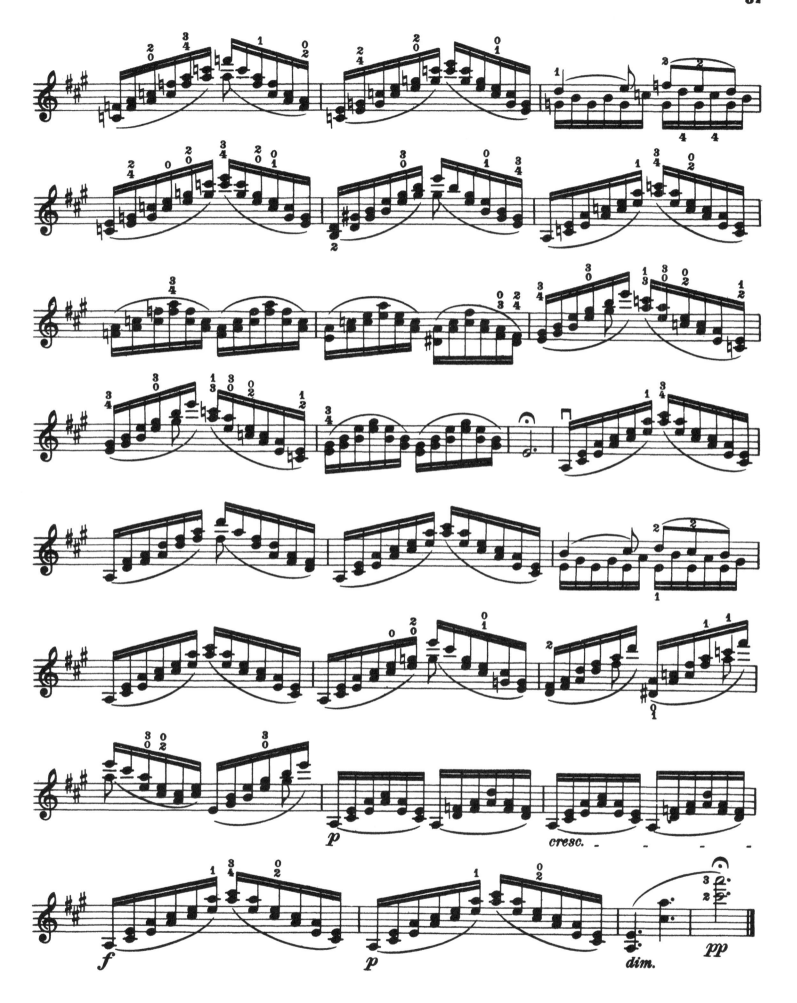

Fantasia
Affettuoso ♩ = 60

24